WHAT A QUESTION!

Opening Doors to Conversation
and
Windows of Discovery

by
Daniel R. Murray

NEW VOYAGE BOOKS
415 Route 18, Suite 234
East Brunswick, NJ 08816

New Voyage Books and *What A Question! Opening Doors to Conversation and Windows of Discovery* are not associated with Workman Publishing or any of its publications, including *The Book of Questions* or *Love and Sex: The Book of Questions.*

Illustrations from the Dover Pictorial Archives Series including *Women: A Pictorial Archive from Nineteenth-Century Sources* by Jim Harter, *Children: A Pictorial Archive from Nineteen-Century Sources* by Carol Belanger Grafton, and *Men: A Pictorial Archive from Nineteenth-Century Sources* by Jim Harter.

Library of Congress Cataloging-in-Publication Data

Murray, Daniel R., 1962-
    What a question! : opening doors to conversation and
windows of discovery / by Daniel R. Murray.
      p. cm.
    ISBN 0-9623408-4-7 : $7.95
    1. Conversation. 2. Self-perception—Problems, exercises, etc.
I. Title.
BJ2121.M88 1989   89-36894
158'.2—dc20   CIP

ATTENTION: ORGANIZATIONS AND CORPORATIONS

Quantity discounts are available on bulk purchases of this book for sales promotions, premiums, or fund-raising. Special books or excerpts can also be created for specific needs. For information, please contact our Special Sales Department, New Voyage Books, 415 Route 18, Suite 234, East Brunswick, NJ 08816, 201-249-7569.

Printed and bound in the United States of America

To Mom and Dad,
    who opened countless doors
    and windows for me.

Acknowledgments

I am indebted to many people who helped in the development of *What A Question!* Each person made a unique and special contribution that was woven into the final fabric of the book.

Many thanks to Tom and Marilyn Ross of About Books, Inc. Their creative suggestions, editorial assistance and vast book publishing experience have been invaluable to the development of this project. I've discovered how much they really do know about books!

I would like to thank those who shared hours of conversation and many thoughts and ideas on the manuscript. Thanks to Craig Jbara, Bette Jbara, Karen Paczas, Kevin Cronin, Bill Stewart, Brad Whittemore, Kevin Yoder, Marty Hogan, Terry and Michelle Murray, Tom and Mim Murray, "Indiana" Joe and Debbie Flanigen, Kevin and Marianne Murray, Beth Shively, Kathleen Hogan, Kathy Brady, and E. C. Gan. Special thanks to Brian Murray whose outlook on life and sense of humor have been an inspiration to me.

My friends from the diner group provided the spark that started me on this quest. Many thanks to "the originals" Jerry Hooben, Kim Stevens, and Sue Imfeld. Also Kevin Wada, Jeff Sung, Leah Sobrepena, Linda Page, and Jackie Ussher. I'm very grateful to Marilyn Jablonski for her encouragement and unending faith throughout this course of this project.

Finally, I would like to offer deep thanks to Gary and Karen Jbara whose dedication, friendship, and hard work were instrumental to the publication of this book.

Foreword

What a Question stimulated long discussions between my wife and me, and between us and our children. It is a superb job of soul-searching and fun-smacking inquiry, often deeply personal and sometimes light and fun—as love relationships ought to be.

As a counseling professional who often works with couples, I find two barriers that hinder effective communication in relationships. The first occurs when partners don't argue effectively and thus avoid bringing up controversy. The second happens when a couple runs out of "things to talk about." This book addresses the latter problem marvelously, and could be used effectively by couples wanting to deepen and intensify their relationship...which is nearly every couple!

What a Question is an impressive volume worthy of the attention of "young" couples up to the age of 93! I eagerly recommend it for its conversation-spawning ability and easygoing style.

Dennis E. Boike, Ph.D.
Boike Marriage, Family, &
Individual Counseling, Inc.
Rochester, New York

Poem for everyman

I will present you
parts
of
my
self
slowly
if you are patient and tender.
I will open drawers
that mostly stay closed
and bring out places and people and things
sounds and smells, loves and frustrations, hopes and
sadnesses,
bits and pieces of three decades of life
that have been grabbed off
in chunks
and found lying in my hands.
they have eaten
their way into my memory,
carved their way into
my heart.
altogether-you or i will never see them-
they are me.

if you regard them lightly,
deny that they are important
or worse, judge them
i will quietly, slowly,
begin to wrap them up,
in small pieces of velvet,
like worn silver and gold jewelry,
tuck them away
in a small wooden chest of drawers
and close.

from *How Do You Feel?* by John Thomas Wood

Table of Contents

Introduction

Somewhere, a group of people are sitting down to talk at a diner. They may look like any other group at any other diner. But, indeed, they are special. They discuss all sorts of interesting, fascinating things. Never ordinary, everyday things. Hopes, dreams, challenges, friendships, memories, thoughts, and feelings. Maybe even romance. Or a once-in-a-lifetime experience never to be forgotten. For those few magical hours everything other than their conversation disappears. When they depart, they feel they know each other a little bit better. And they even know themselves better. Maybe they leave feeling a little bit taller than when they came. And they look forward to their next conversation just a little bit more.

The secret of success of the group lies primarily in having a reservoir of intriguing questions to ask. And a few other things, such as openness, honesty, willingness to listen, and respect for each other's feelings.

A thoughtful question is like a fine painting. It is so simple it can disarm you. But it is also very deep and complex at the same time. Reflecting on a penetrating question enables you to explore new paths of self-discovery on an introspective journey. It conjures up feelings, memories, and images that just seem to effortlessly float into your mind. And it can help you share those feelings, memories, and images with those who are close to you. It often nudges forth subtle revelations that can inspire a conversation on to exciting, new highs.

So, get ready to embark on an exciting journey. You will learn some very interesting things about your friends, your family, and especially yourself. Marvelous, wonderful things. Even surprising things. You'll laugh. You'll be touched. Your jaw may even drop once or twice. But it's all part of great conversation. And it's all waiting for you. Just turn the page...

Part I

It's a Wonderful Life

Getting to Know You

1. You are standing in line
   behind the Tin Man, the
   Scarecrow, and the Cowardly Lion
   waiting for the Wizard of Oz
   to appear.

   Assuming you already have
   a heart, a brain,
   and sufficient courage,
   what would you ask the Wizard
   for?

2. Which of the following
would you rather be assigned:

A loosely defined, open-ended task
that allows you to choose your
own approach?

Or a well defined task that can
only be accomplished in one
manner?

Why?

3. Would you call yourself a risk-taker?

Do you tend to have friends who
take risks or play it safe?

4. Are you a spontaneous person?

    If so, give an example of the last
    time you did something completely
    on the spur of the moment.

    How did it turn out?

5. Finish the sentence:

    "I am most happy when..."

6. Do you enjoy surprises?

    What has been the single biggest
    surprise of your life?

7. How much confidence
   do you have in yourself?

   In which three people
   do you have the most confidence?

8. How would you hope to be described
   to someone who doesn't know you,
   but whom you will soon meet?

9. Are you good
   at making compromises?

   What, in your view, does it take to
   make a good compromise?

10. Do you often feel competitive?

What activity or person brings out the competitor in you?

11. What would instantly cheer you up when you're feeling down?

12. What is your best time of day?

Do you start slowly and build up speed throughout the day?

Or start with high energy in the morning and gradually wind down as the day goes on?

13. What assumptions might someone make about you if they were to see only your room, your desk, or some personal area where you keep your things?

Would these assumptions be accurate?

14. How did you like growing up in your particular family?

In what ways was your family different from others in the area?

How has that difference impacted your life?

15. If you could adopt one personality trait from a famous person, which person and trait would you choose?

16. In the movie *The Sound of Music*, Julie Andrews sings about some of her favorite things.

    What items would be on a list of your favorite things?

17. Do you have good intuition?

    Give an example of a time when your intuition was particularly good—

    Other than when you decided to buy this book.

18. Have you ever firmly resolved to do
     something and decided
     beforehand you absolutely would
     not fail?

     Describe that experience.

     What was the outcome?

19. You walk into a bookstore
     to browse for a new book.

     In which section of the bookstore
     would you begin?

     Which sections would you ignore
     completely?

20. If left to your own devices,
    would you choose to wake up early
    or late every day?

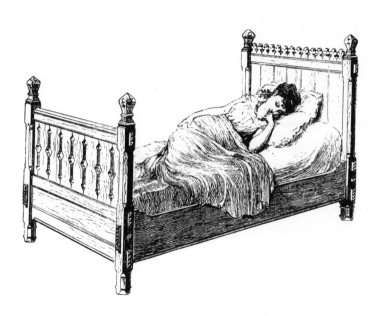

The Way We Were

21. What is the first memory that pops into your mind when you hear each of these words:

   Cotton candy?

   Thanksgiving?

   First day of school?

   Double dare? Summer vacation?

   Trick or treat?

   Weekly allowance?

22. What did your family talk about
     at the dinner table when you were
     growing up?

23. If possible, would you edit
     and improve the story line
     in one chapter of your life?

    Which chapter would you change
    and how would you alter it?

24. Using a one-word description,
     characterize yourself at some
     younger age.

    Does that word still apply to you
    today?

25. In the past year,
    when have you felt exuberant?

26. What radio or television show
    do you fondly remember from
    your childhood?

27. Is there anyone
    you wish you had gotten to know
    better?

    Why did you want to know him or
    her better?

    What prevented this from
    happening?

28. Are you a sentimental person?

    Which of the following makes you feel sentimental or nostalgic:

    Weddings?

    Golden oldie songs?

    Old letters from a former sweetheart?

    A high school yearbook?

    Graduations?

    Reunions?

    Photo albums?

    Or something else?

29. In which areas do you grade
your parents favorably in the way
they brought you up?

30. What is the greatest opportunity
you ever seized?

Did you realize at the time the
importance of that opportunity?

31. Picture yourself as a teenager.

What things about you have not
changed since then?

What has changed the most?

32. What memory is evoked by
    the word "safety" for you?

    How about "warmth"?

33. Describe your circle of friends
    from a past school or job.

    How did they influence you during
    that time of your life?

34. What was your favorite toy
    when you were a child?

    What is your favorite toy now?

35. Have you lived through
    any experience that has
    dramatically changed you
    or your life?

36. Describe a fond holiday memory
    you cherish.

    Which holiday has the most
    memories attached to it?

37. When have you "burned a bridge"
    behind you?

    Did burning the bridge help or
    hurt you?

    Did you ever wish you could go
    back across that bridge?

The New You

38. In which field of endeavor
    would you most enjoy becoming
    skillful or knowledgeable?

39. When changes take place
    in your life, do they tend to occur
    gradually or suddenly?

    Give a recent example.

40. If your life were portrayed as a movie, would it be:

A comedy?

A drama?

An action/adventure?

A romance?

Or a documentary?

Which actor or actress would portray you?

How long would it be a box office hit?

What would it be rated?

41. Which feeling or emotion
do you rarely experience?

Which of the following would you
like to feel more often:

Impulsive?

Thrilled?

Inspired?

Tender?

Passionate?

Bold?

Ecstatic?

42. Name three personal high points
in the past year.

Predict some high points for the
coming year.

43. What do you like most
about yourself?

How do people who know you well
describe you?

What would they say is your best
trait, other than modesty?

44. In life, what do you approach
with the most enthusiasm or
passion?

45. When someone you meet says,
"I've heard a lot about you,"
what do you imagine
they have heard?

46. Describe what it is like to be you.

What are some unique factors
that make you different from
everyone else?

47. What goal in life would you pursue
if you were guaranteed you
couldn't fail?

48. If you compare last week
    to being at bat in a baseball game,
    which most closely describes your
    performance:

    A ground ball?

    Single?

    Walk to first?

    Hit by a wild pitch?

    Sacrifice fly?

    Foul ball?

    Triple?

    Strike out?

    Home run?

When was your last grand slam
home run?

49. Do you generally set high,
     medium, or low expectations for
     yourself?

    For your best friend?

50. Which of the following words
    describe you when you are
    at your best?

    Funny

    Carefree

    Exciting

    Interesting

    Playful

    Creative

    Adventurous

    Romantic

    High-spirited

    All of the above

Friends and Acquaintances

51. Are you willing to ask for advice from others?

What is the best advice you have ever been given?

Are you often asked by others for your advice?

52. How is talking to someone on the telephone different for you than a face-to-face conversation?

    Do you prefer the telephone for any types of conversations?

53. Is it easy for you to demonstrate affection to the special people in your life?

54. What does true friendship mean to you?

    Define the difference between a friend and an acquaintance.

55. Would you prefer attending a large party with many new faces?

Or a smaller gathering where you knew most of the people?

56. Name a close friend from the past whom you no longer see very often.

Describe your friendship and what you enjoyed doing together.

What is your most fond memory of that person?

57. You are planning an extended vacation and want to take someone along.

What type of person is best suited to be your travel companion?

Specifically, what would this person add to the trip?

58. What qualities in a friend are most important to you?

Are these qualities the same in both a male and female friend?

Or somewhat different?

59. With whom do you most enjoy
     spending time?

     Why?

60. Has anyone ever inspired you
     to do something you considered to
     be beyond your capabilities?

61. Who is the most unforgettable
     person you've ever met?

62. How many people really know you?

    Do you include yourself in
    this group?

    Who knows you best?

63. When saying good-bye to a close
    friend because of a relocation,

    Is it easier for you to be the one
    going away?

    Or the one staying behind?

    Why?

Would You...?

64. You are happily reading
    War and Peace while standing in a
    long line to renew your driver's
    license.

    You notice someone cut in line
    just behind you.

    Would you say something or stay
    quiet?

    What if they cut in just ahead of
    you?

65. Suppose you are offered
    a once-in-a-lifetime career
    opportunity that involves moving to
    France for the next three years.

    Would you accept?

    Parlez-vous francais?

66. Would you prefer to be in a
    competition in which you could
    quite easily win, but would bring
    little acclaim?

    Or one in which you were the long
    shot, but would bring national
    fame if you won?

67. Your entire family has not been together for several years.

A reunion, which has been planned for many months, is two weeks away.

You win a free nontransferable trip to a tropical island for the same weekend as the reunion.

Would you choose fun in the sun or Aunt Peg's potato salad?

68. Would you rather go on a well-planned trip with an established itinerary?

Or one that was very loosely planned and allowed you freedom to do what you would like?

Why?

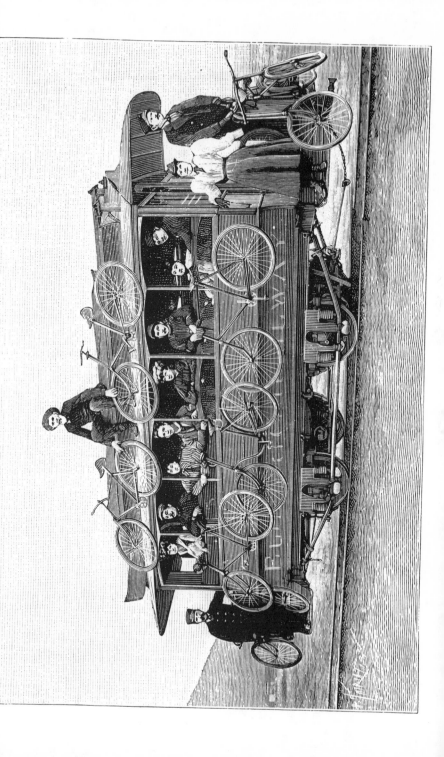

69. An eminent adventurer/archaeologist
    invites you to accompany him on
    his next mission to Peru.

    Would you accept?

    What would you take along?

70. As you are passing through
    Chatfield, Minnesota, your car
    coughs a cloud of smoke and
    stops.

    While waiting for the mechanic to
    repair your engine:

    Would you wander around town
    and start a conversation with some
    local people?

    Simply sit in the service station
    and read USA Today?

71. You are visiting Athens with a close friend who unexpectedly becomes sick and must stay in the hotel room for the duration of your trip.

Due to heavy bookings, you are not able to get a flight home for another week.

Your friend urges you to tour the city and enjoy your vacation.

Would you go out and have fun or spend the week in the hotel room at your friend's side?

Explain the reasoning behind your decision.

Part II

Just for Fun

Crystal Ball Gazing

72. If you could have only one guarantee in life,

    What would it be?

73. What are you awaiting with the most anticipation?

    Do you wish you could turn the clock forward to that time?

74. How would you want to be awakened
    tomorrow morning to start the day
    off right?

75. What is on your list
of "Things I would like to do
someday...?"

76. What talents or abilities of yours
have not yet been fully
developed?

77. What natural ability
do you wish you had?

What magical power do you wish
you could have?

How would you utilize that power?

78. How often do you think about the future?

At those times, what feeling or emotion do you most commonly experience?

Is the future exciting to you?

79. If you could write your next fortune cookie message, what would it say?

What would you ask?

80. Describe a situation that would be "paradise on earth" for you.

81. If you could travel back through history, which time and place would you visit?

    If you could interview any person in history, whom would you choose?

82. If you were granted a wish for any person other than yourself:

    Whom would you choose to give it to?

    What would you wish for that person?

83. If you wrote your autobiography:

What would you name the chapters?

Which ones would be the most interesting?

What would be the title of the book?

84. Describe your dream home.

What mood or feeling would a visitor experience upon entering this house?

85. What could happen tomorrow
that would make your life more
exciting?

86. Describe how you envision
your life changing over the next
few years.

What opportunity do you hope to
have during that time?

On the Lighter Side

87. Do you still believe in Santa Claus?

    If yes, cite evidence to support your belief.

    Has anyone ever told you differently?

88. What is the funniest blooper you are still willing to admit?

89. What food did you especially enjoy
    as a child?

    What food did you especially enjoy
    launching off your plate like a
    projectile?

90. Do you ever sneak extra items
    through the express checkout lane
    at the supermarket?

91. When, if ever, do you feel frisky?

    Are these feelings ever
    accompanied by an inexplicable
    craving for cat food?

92. Do you have enough fun
in your life?

Is it possible to have too much
fun?

What types of enjoyable activities
would you like to experience
more often?

93. What was your best vacation?

Can you remember a vacation
experience that was a fiasco at the
time, but you laughed about later?

94. Does your personality change
    when you get behind the wheel of
    an automobile?

    How about a bumper car at an
    amusement park?

95. What makes you laugh the most?

    When was the last time you really
    laughed hard?

    Whose sense of humor most
    closely matches your own?

96. Can you think of a humorous
    situation in your life when a
    shortage of cash caused you to
    find an unusual way to accomplish
    your objectives?

97. Did you ever skip school to do something fun?

At work, have you recently called in sick, even though you felt fine?

Were the fish biting?

98. If someone who knows you well had to describe you as a certain animal, which one might they choose?

Why?

Would they be more inclined to take this animal in as a family pet or round up a posse to hunt it down?

99. What is the funniest part of a movie
you've ever seen?

Grab Bag

100. What famous person is especially deserving of their fame?

101. What has been your best experience on a team or in a group working towards a common goal?

Were you the leader of the team or group?

102. What gift did you receive
that you will always remember?

Is there presently something you
would be delighted to receive as a
gift, but probably would not buy
on your own?

103. Have you ever discovered something
you took for granted at the time,
but then appreciated after it was
gone?

What do you currently take for
granted?

104. After watching a movie or reading a book, have you ever said, "I can truly relate to the character in that story?"

If so, who was the character and why could you especially identify with him or her?

105. Is it easy for you to adapt to change?

Do you tend to prefer periods with change or times when things remain the same?

106. What is your definition of chivalry?

Have you personally experienced
chivalry anytime in the past three
months?

107. You are planning a dinner
in the most romantic setting
imaginable.

What elements are most important
in achieving a romantic mood?

108. Are you good at thinking up
new ideas?

When are you most creative?

Describe a clever idea you have
come up with lately.

109. How adventurous are you?

What would you ask someone to
do if you wanted to determine
their A.Q., or "adventure
quotient"?

110. What is your favorite line
or scene from a movie?

111. What amount do you consider
to be a lot of money?

How much money would you need
to consider yourself rich?

Can one be rich without a large
amount of money?

112. Is there anything you regret
     doing—or not doing—
     so far in your life?

113. What is the most universally
     experienced emotion?

     What emotion do you most
     commonly experience?

114. Who were your heroes or heroines
     when you were younger?

     Who are your heroes or heroines
     now?

115. How would you prefer to spend an evening if given these choices:

Curled up with a good book at home?

Socializing with friends or relatives?

Meeting new people at an organization you have recently joined?

116. What does a vacation mean to you?

What constitutes the perfect vacation?

117. Which political issues
     being debated today
     will most affect everyday life
     fifty years from now?

118. In your opinion, who is the most
     glamorous woman in the world?

     The most handsome man?

119. If it was available,
     would you take a pill
     in the morning that would fulfill all
     nutritional requirements for the
     day, thereby making it unnecessary
     to eat for twenty-four hours?

120. Are you adept at negotiating
     with others?

Are you more often a hard
bargainer or a fair negotiator?

121. What is the most remarkable coincidence you've ever experienced?

122. Of all the advertisements you've ever seen or heard,

Which one do you most clearly remember?

Why?

123. In what ways is the world a better place today than when you grew up?

What modern day trend do you find most interesting?

124. What comes easier to you
than to most people?

What comes more difficult?

What If?

125. You wake up alone on the beach
    of a lush tropical island after
    miraculously surviving a shipwreck.

    Drums can be faintly heard beating
    from a distant corner of the island.

    Assuming you are not hearing a
    rowdy Club Med party, what would
    be your next move?

126. You are the queen or king
of a small European monarchy in
the Middle Ages.

What would be the quality of life
for the average peasant in your
kingdom?

What type of ruler would you be?

127. You are snowed in for a week
at a mountain ski lodge,
unable to return home.

After overcoming your initial
depression about missing the extra
week of work—

Whom or what would you like to
have with you to make it a
pleasant week?

128. Your job entails driving
     a refrigerated lobster truck
     from the coast of Maine
     to Odebolt, Iowa.

     Halfway through the trip,
     on a sweltering August day,
     the refrigeration unit in your truck
     suddenly fails.

     All repair shops are closed
     for the weekend and the cargo will
     certainly spoil before you reach
     your destination.

     What will you do?

129. If you had a wristwatch
     which would beep as a warning
     five minutes before someone was
     about to hurt your feelings, how
     would you use it?

130. You buy a stereo at a store
     that posts a large sign reading,
     "No refunds, returns or exchanges.
     All sales final."

When you get home and turn the
stereo on, it doesn't work properly.

You go back to the store with the
defective merchandise and the
manager rudely says, "Didn't you
read the sign? I'm sorry, I can't
help you. Go away."

How would you respond?

Would your response change if he
said, in a courteous and apologetic
tone, "I'm very sorry and I would
love to help you out, but the
owner is quite stubborn and will
not budge on this policy."

131. You are offered one of the following three historical jobs. Which would you take and why?

    1)   The lookout on Christopher Columbus' ship

    2)   A knight of King Arthur's Round Table at Camelot

    3)   The chief strategic military advisor to Napoleon

132. You wander away from your Bolivian tour guide and are lost in the jungle for ten years.

What is the first thing you would do upon returning to civilization (After taking a shower, of course)?

133. After entering a short story contest, you are delighted to learn you have been selected as the winner.

You soon discover, however, the winning story is not the one you submitted.

Apparently, your name was mistakenly placed on an anonymous submission and you receive the $10,000 prize check in the mail.

Assuming you are the only one to know about the error and you're reasonably confident it will never be discovered, what would you do?

134. If you suddenly became financially independent, how would your life change?

135. You take over as coach of the local
     high school soccer team.

     The team has suffered through
     three losing seasons and everyone
     expects yet another disastrous year.

     How would you approach the job?

     What advice would you give to the
     team?

     Would it be important to you that
     the team have a winning season
     under your direction?

136. You are placed in charge
     of making the world a perfect
     place, then given great power.

     What is the first change you would
     institute?

137. You have the opportunity to teach
a third grade class for two weeks.

What one specific thing would you
teach the class that you hope
would leave a lifetime impression
on them?

138. Next weekend, you and three friends
want to get away and have fun.

If you had less than $60 total to
spend, what might you decide to
do?

What if the amount of money you
had for the weekend was
unlimited?

139. If there were a special pill
     that could help you either establish
     or break any habit you choose—

What habit would you select to
establish or break?

140. If you had a boat that was your
     home and a dependable source of
     income—

In which part of the world would
you go to live?

Does this lifestyle appeal to you?

Tantalizers

141. Have you ever said
   or thought to yourself,
   "I will never do that again"?

   Did you ever do it again?

142. If you could remove one word
     from the language, which one
     would you eliminate?

     Why?

143. Have you ever accomplished
     something which at first seemed
     impossible?

144. How did the birth order in your
     family affect your personality?

     How would you be different if you
     had traded places with an older or
     younger sibling?

     Would you make such a trade?

145. Think of your personal strengths
     as making up a long chain.

   Which link is strongest?
   (If your chain happens to be less
   than three links, you may entirely
   disregard this question.)

146. Have you ever felt invincible?

   When?

147. How do you define creativity?

   How do you personally express
   your creativity?

148. Think of a person
who greatly influences you.

What aspect of your personality
has been in some way formed by
knowing this person?

149. What items would you place
in a time capsule that would give
some future generation a clear
picture of what your life is like?

150. How concerned are you
with the feelings of other people?

Are there times when you must
ignore the feelings of others to do
something important for yourself?

151. What is your most prized possession
     that money can buy?

     That money cannot buy?

     Which has greater value to you?

152. Imagine that a friend
     you highly respect and trust
     tells you he or she
     personally witnessed a phenomena
     you previously did not believe
     was possible.

     How would you decide
     whether or not
     to believe your friend?

153. You are just launching
into a new activity
and somebody says to you,
"You'll never be able to do that."

Would this discourage you
or cause you to grit your teeth
and try even harder?

Does your response depend on
who made the comment?

154. Which of the following
most appeals to you as an
enjoyable way to spend a day:

Hike up a mountain and see a
beautiful sunset?

Attend a baseball game?

Go out to eat at a restaurant and
see a movie afterwards?

155. While inventing the light bulb,
    Thomas Edison tried
    over ten thousand approaches
    before he finally succeeded.

    If you had been in his place,
    how many times would you have
    tried before giving up?

    In your experience,
    do you find Edison's level
    of persistence in your circle of
    friends or work associates?

156. Do you believe
    in supernatural episodes?

    Have you ever experienced
    something you believe
    to be supernatural?

157. A friend of yours
has done something that violates
one of your principles.

Do you stand up for your belief
and risk offending your friend?

Or simply let the incident pass?

158. What ideas did you learn
from your parents as you grew up
that you have since discarded or
replaced with new ideas?

159. When you play a game, do you
play to win or just to have fun?

Part III

Guys and Dolls

Battle of the Sexes

160. What are the keys
     to being a successful:

   Husband or father?

   Wife or mother?

   How do you define "successful" in
   this context?

161. What is the current stereotype
of members of your gender?

How are you different
from this stereotype?

162. What do you believe
women are inherently better
at doing than men?

What are men better at
than women?

163. Who are the most outstanding
women of our time?

The most outstanding men?

164. How do you feel about
     "beauty" pageants?

     Would you encourage your
     daughter to enter one?

165. What general personal qualities
     do you most admire about
     members of the opposite sex?

     What makes a person sexy to you?

166. Suppose you were a member
     of the opposite sex for one day
     and you happened to meet
     your current self.

     What would you like
     about your personality?

167. Which traits do you
     think of as being feminine?

     Masculine?

     Not associated with either gender?

168. Do you have better
     conversations with women or men?

     How are these discussions
     different?

169. What would you like
     members of the opposite sex
     to admire most about you?

170. Is there a double standard
in the way men and women are
treated or expected to behave?

171. If you could change one quality or
behavior about the opposite sex—

What would it be?

Is there anything
you would change about
members of your own sex?

172. Do men's expectations vary from
women's concerning marriage?

If so, how?

173. Are there any privileges
accorded to women on the sole
basis that they are women?

Does the same hold true for men?

If so, what is your opinion of
these?

Singles Game

174. What type of first date
would make you want to continue
dating someone?

175. Describe what you expect
from a dating relationship.

What would be the ideal?

176. You have been dating Person A
for five months and your
relationship is smooth but
somewhat uneventful.

One day you learn that Person B,
whom you have always liked, is
very interested in you and very
available.

Even if there are no problems with
A, would you break up and go out
with B instead?

If so, what would you tell
Person A?

177. In your relationships
have you more often been
the "pursuer" or the "pursued"?

Is there necessarily a pursuer and
a pursued in every relationship?

178. Do you ever look at your date
     and think to yourself—

     "Would he or she be a good
     marriage partner?"

     If so, how long does it take
     after you meet someone for this
     question to cross your mind?

179. If you could have a date with
      any eligible person in the world—

      Whom would you choose?

      Where would you go on the date?

180. Do you believe, as the saying goes,
      "all is fair in love and war"?

181. Are there any social pressures
      on single people to get married?

      If so, does this pressure vary
      depending on one's gender?

182. Can you recall your first date?

What do you most remember
about the experience?

183. How are courtship and dating
different now than they were
in the 1950s?

Have they changed for the better?

184. Do you have above-average
or average standards in choosing
whom you would like to date?

Have your standards changed in
the past two years?

If so, how?

185. Your best friend sets you up
for a blind date next weekend.

Would you rather be told your
date is extremely good-looking or
that he or she has a great personality and is a terrific person?

186. Have you ever been infatuated
with someone?

How long (months, days, or
milliseconds) did it last?

187. Do you prefer knowing someone as a
friend before dating him or her?

Would you rather date one person
exclusively or be free to go on
dates with different people?

188. Would you rather date someone
     who is exciting and full of intrigue
     and surprises or someone more
     down-to-earth whom you could
     envision being a great friend
     through good times and bad?

189. Which of the following song titles
     could sum up your love life and
     why?

     "The Wanderer"

     "You Can't Always
        Get What You Want"

     "Lightning Strikes"

     "Ain't Too Proud To Beg"

     "This Magic Moment"

     "My Eyes Adored You"

190. Your son is about to go
on his first date.

What would you tell him to
prepare him for this experience?

How would you advise your
daughter before her first date?

191. Do you prefer to plan
what you will do on a date, have it
planned by your partner, or just
make it up as you go along?

What is the most fun you have
ever had on a date?

What makes a good date?

That Special Someone

192. What is important for you
     to know about your partner
     before marriage?

193. How career-oriented
     versus family-oriented
     would you like your spouse to be?

194. At what point is a person
        truly ready to be married?

     Should age be a major factor in
     one's readiness?

195. At the outset
        of a romantic relationship,
        do you generally have an idea
        in mind of the direction you would
        like to see the relationship go?

     Or do you simply wait and see
     how it turns out?

196. Have you ever fallen in love?

     Describe, if you can, the feeling
     you experienced.

197. You are happily surprised
     on your birthday with a gift
     of a "personal coupon" booklet
     from your special someone.

     Each page is redeemable
     for a different favor or treat
     from that person.

     What personal coupons would you
     like to see in the booklet?

     (Note: This question has been
     granted a PG-13 rating by the
     Conversation Ratings Association.)

198. What does it mean to you
     to be vulnerable in a relationship?

     Does vulnerability help
     or hurt a relationship?

199. In what ways would you like
     your partner's personality
     to be similar to yours?

     In what ways different?

     Do opposites really attract?

200. In a romance, do you believe
     the person who is less interested
     also has the most control over the
     progress of the relationship?

     If so, do you find this ironic?

201. What are the most important
     characteristics you would cherish
     in a marriage partner?

     Which one stands above the rest?

202. What are the key elements
     of an exciting and passionate
     relationship?

203. You have been going together
     with your special someone
     for two years.

     Although you're not yet engaged
     to be married, you think this might
     happen sometime during the next
     year.

     Unexpectedly, your partner
     is transferred in his or her job
     to a city 1000 miles away.

     How would you react
     to this new development?

     What choices
     would you be forced to make?

204. In a romantic relationship,
how much do you desire free time
spent away from your lover?

Does spending time away
from each other strengthen
or weaken a relationship?

How important is maintaining your
individuality in a relationship?

205. What aspect of single life
will be the most difficult to give up
when you get married?

What are the benefits of marriage?

Do they outweigh the
disadvantages?

206. What is your definition of love?

Have your relationships generally
fulfilled this definition?

207. You are qualifying someone
as a possible marriage partner
but can ask only one question.

What would you ask?

For Better...
or for Worse

208. What factor is crucial
     in sustaining a lifelong relationship
     with another person?

209. What did you learn about marriage
     from watching your parents that
     turned out to be particularly
     helpful in your own marriage?

210. As a newlywed couple,
    you and your spouse are evaluating
    job offers and choosing
    where to locate.

    You have an unexciting job offer
    in the city where your in-laws live,
    but much better offers in a city
    300 miles away.

    Which would hold a greater appeal
    for you?

    How important would your
    spouse's opinion be
    in making a final decision?

211. When is it okay
    to keep secrets from your spouse?

212. With regard to question number 210,
imagine you are now the in-laws
and your son or daughter with
spouse are weighing these same
choices.

Would you prefer they seek the
best possible job or live near you?

213. What is the best way
for a married couple to handle
their financial situation?

Should there be limitations placed
on each partner regarding the
spending of money?
How often should this topic be
discussed?

Is there "his and hers" money or
"our" money?

214. Name one of your expectations
       about marriage that has changed
       since getting married.

215. Are there any characteristics
       the happily married couples
       you know share in common?

     If so, what are these traits?

216. If you traded places with your spouse
       and assumed all of his or her
       responsibilities—

     Would you be happy?

     What is the greatest adjustment
     you would have to make?

217. You attend a company award
        ceremony and share stimulating
        conversation all evening with an
        attractive, single co-worker of the
        opposite sex.

        Would you tell your spouse,
        who was not in attendance,
        about this facet of the dinner?

        Why?

        Why not?

218. What do you like most
        about being married?

        What has been the hardest
        adjustment you've had to make?

219. What opportunities
does marriage create?

What limitations does it bring?

220. Is your spouse the person
you can most easily confide in?

For which topics would your
answer change?

221. What is your idea
of the perfect marriage?

Do you know any couples who
personify this ideal?

222. Is flirting a harmless activity
     for married people
     or something to be avoided?

223. How is your marriage different
     now than it was shortly after you
     were married?

The Patter
of Little Feet

224. Your child somehow is not doing
as well in school as you or the
teacher thinks he or she can.

At the parent-teacher conference
you learn that your child's friends
may be having a detrimental effect
on his or her performance.

What would you do?

225. How does a marriage change
with the arrival of children?

226. At what age would you
let your daughter begin dating?

Your son?

If you indicated different ages,
explain why.

227. Your child goes away for
a two-week visit to summer camp.

After only three days,
he or she calls and tearfully asks
for a ride home.

What would you do?

228. Imagine you are a parent and
one of your children seems to be
gifted in an area such as
gymnastics or music.

To what extent would you devote
the resources of the family
to make sure this talent
gets fully developed?

229. What principle did you learn
from your parents that you hope
to pass along to your children?

230. Is sibling rivalry constructive?

If your children were extremely
competitive with each other would
you attempt to intervene?

231. If you already have children,
what has been your most satisfying
moment as a mother or father?

232. If given the choice,
would you prefer raising
a small or large family?

Growing up in a small
or large family?

What factors enter these decisions?

233. What is the best way for parents
to avoid favoring one child over
another?

Is it possible to raise a family
without ever showing favoritism?

Part IV

The Rational Inquirer

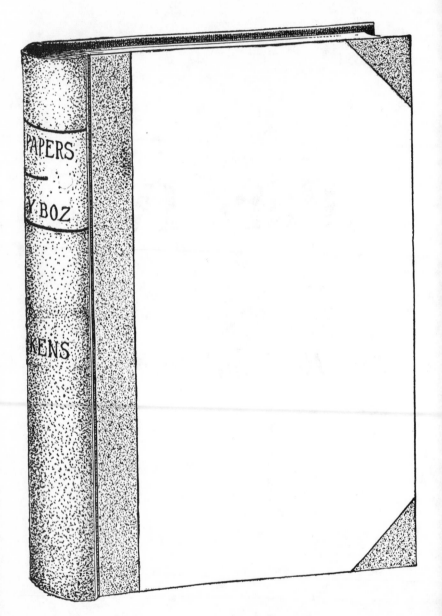

Fireside Chats

234. Has there ever been a time
    in your life you later considered
    a "turning point"?

235. Have you ever read a book
    or seen a movie that permanently
    changed you?

236. Name one thing someone learns
about you only after knowing you
for a long time.

237. What period of your life
has been the happiest?

238. What are your highest
priorities in life?

What principle(s) do you value
the most?

239. What has been one of the peak
experiences in your life?

240. Is human nature basically
     good or evil?

     Do you view the world as a
     friendly or unfriendly place?

     What influenced you
     to form these views?

241. What currently motivates
     you the most?

     Do you suppose this will still be
     the case fifteen years from now?

242. Do you evaluate a day
     based on how much you enjoyed it
     or how much you accomplished?

243. Do you ever take uninterrupted
quiet time for reflection,
thought, or meditation?

If so, what is the greatest benefit
you experience from this time?

244. Do you think more about—

Goals, plans, and ambitions?

People, feelings, and relationships?

245. If you could choose to
have been born in another era—

What era would you pick?

Why?

246. What is your definition of success?

What is the secret of success?

247. Do you have a good balance
of activities and priorities
in your life?

If you had to suggest one area
of your life that might be
out of balance, which would it be?

248. So far, have things turned out
in your life pretty much
as you expected?

As you wanted?

249. What is the primary motivator
     in your personal relationships?

250. What is your definition of romance?

    Describe a scene
    or situation you have experienced
    that was very romantic.

    Which song
    is most romantic for you?

251. Is there anything you are not
     able to convey or communicate
     with words to another person?

    How do you attempt to convey
    or communicate such things?

252. What lasting impact has your mother
     had on your life?

   Your father?

253. If you could travel
     back through history and bring one
     thing forward to the present day,
     what would you bring?

254. What factors have most formed
     your personality?

255. When were the "good ol' days"
     in your life?

256. Who is the most brilliant person
   you have ever met?

   The most artistic?

   The most philosophical?

   The most similar to you?

Workaday World

257. You have been struggling
with a complex problem at work
and it is time to make a decision.

Your analysis and your logical
mind tell you one thing but your
"gut feel" tells you the opposite.

Which do you listen to?

258. How did you choose
     your line of work?

     If you were to do it over again,
     would you make the same career
     choices as you did the first time
     around?

259. What type of reward do you most appreciate for your work?

Is money more important to you than job satisfaction?

260. After a bad day at work—

Do you prefer to talk about what upset you?

Do something to take your mind off it?

Be completely left alone?

261. How many work days, out of 100, would you call bad days?

262. You are vice president
     of a manufacturing company.

     The chairman of the board,
     to your delight, promotes you
     to president.

     One of your new duties
     is to sign off on reports
     which you soon discover are often
     misleading or dishonest.

     There is heavy pressure on you to
     maintain the status quo and not
     rock the boat.

     What would you do?

263. What one piece of advice
     would you give to someone
     just starting a job
     where you presently work?

264. As the founder
of a growing company, you decide
it is time to write a statement of
your company's philosophy.

What principles are the best ones
to build a solid business upon?

265. What characteristics
would your ideal job have?

How many of these are present in
your current position?

266. If you could be qualified
for a new career by next year,
what career would you choose?

267. Would you rather be voted "most respected" or "most popular" within your circle of co-workers?

If you were a supervisor, would you prefer your people like or respect you?

Why?

268. What has been your favorite job?

Your most satisfying work experience?

Who has been the best boss you ever worked for?

Why?

188

269. On a project at work,
would you rather be responsible—

For some specific, important
details that need to be done?

For coordinating the whole project
which entails constantly looking at
the "big picture"?

270. While working late into the night
on your company's computer,
you accidentally discover
a confidential memo that says you
are one of twelve employees due
to be terminated in one month.

What would you do with this
information?

271. Does your work cause stress
in your life?

If so, what constructive ways have
you found to "blow off steam"?

272. A gas station you work for
has a strict policy
of a minimum $5 purchase.

The manager has made it
crystal clear you will be fired
if you break policy even once.

One winter night at 11 p.m.
a stranded motorist with only $2
walks up to your station
carrying an empty gas can.

What will you do?

Will your decision change if the
manager is watching you?

273. Your company announces a plan
     where at age 35 you are offered
     a temporary retirement
     of 10 years,
     after which you return to work.

     You make up the time
     by working 10 years past
     the normal retirement age.

     What would you think of this
     plan?

     Would you take it
     if you became eligible?

274. On an important project at work,
     do you prefer to work—

     Independently?

     As part of a team?

275. One day at work you make
a brilliant discovery you are sure
will revolutionize your company.

You are dismayed to find,
however, no one will listen to you.

What would you do?

276. Which of the following jobs
most appeals to you?

Social worker
helping disadvantaged children.

Stockbroker earning a large salary.

Well-known mayor of a small city.

277. Who has had the greatest impact
     on you in your work life?

278. What is the funniest thing
     that has ever happened to you
     at work?

279. There is a 10-person team
     competing with a 200-person team
     to develop a new product
     within your company.

     If given the choice, which team
     would you join?

     Why?

Handle with Care

280. Does any particular song
make you feel sad?

Do you prefer to hear this song
once in awhile anyway?

If yes, why?

281. Have you ever had an experience
      that initially seemed unlucky,
      turn out to be lucky?

      Have you ever suffered a loss
      or failure that helped you
      at some later point in life?

282. What is difficult for you
      to say to another person?

      (Supercalifragilisticexpialidocious
      does not count as a valid answer.)

283. When was the last time
      you realized you were wrong
      about something?

      Were you able to openly admit it?

284. Have you ever been heartbroken?

How long did it take you
to fully recover?

285. Do you prefer to talk to someone
when you are upset with them
or wait until after you've cooled
off awhile?

286. Have you ever experienced déja vu —
the feeling you have previously
experienced an event that has just
now occurred?

Describe the incident.

287. Describe a special memory
closely linked to a specific feeling,
such as excitement or tranquility.

Does that feeling return
when you relive the memory?

288. What has been the most difficult
decision you ever had to make?

Did you make the correct choice?

289. Do you tend to−

Thrive on pressure?

Avoid it at all costs?

290. Do you cry at movies?

   If not, do you make an effort
   to hold back the tears?

   Why?

291. Can you remember
   a painful but important lesson
   you learned in the past?

292. What is the most challenging
   undertaking you ever attempted?

   (Those who have climbed Mt.
   Everest need not answer this one;
   we will make an assumption.)

293. To what cause, if any,
     are you most committed?

    On what issue
    currently being debated
    do you have the strongest feelings?

    What is your position
    on that issue?

294. Can you think of anything
     that used to scare you
     but no longer does?

    How did you overcome this fear?

295. Describe a feeling or emotion
     you hope
     you will never experience.

296. If someone met you
for only 15 minutes,
what impressions might they form
about you?

Would these be accurate
or inaccurate?

Have you ever seriously misjudged
someone by first impression, then
revised your view of them later?

On what basis do you initially
judge people?

297. Have you ever said to yourself:

"I can't believe
this is happening to me"?

When?

298. Have you ever felt powerless
to influence the outcome
of a situation in which you
were involved?

299. How do you handle criticism?

300. Can an argument
have a healthy outcome?

In an argument are you—

A diplomat?

A trained boxer?

A guerrilla ambush fighter?

Grand Finale

301. Who is the most beautiful
     or handsome person you ever met?

     What features or characteristics,
     in your opinion, comprise physical
     beauty?

302. Have you ever had an experience
     you hoped would never end?

303. What has been
    the single greatest advancement
    in the history of mankind?

304. When was the first time in your life
     you felt truly independent?

What constitutes independence?

305. In 25 words or less,
     what is the meaning of life?

306. What do you consider to be
     the three most important factors
     that foster quality of life?

307. If you could go back in your life and
thank someone for helping you—

Whom would you go back
and thank?

How did that person assist you?

308. What adds the most excitement
to your life?

What gives you the most
satisfaction?

309. If you could be a little kid again
for only one day,
how would you spend that day?

310. Where does money fit
        into your set of priorities?

    What do you consider
    to be more important than money?

311. If you were given
        two extra hours per day—

    How would you use this bonus
    time?

312. Do you believe
        ultimately there is justice
        in the world?

    Why?

    Why not?

313. How often in the course of a week
      are you intellectually challenged?

      Physically challenged?

      If given the choice,
        would you prefer—

      An intellectual challenge?

      A physical challenge?

314. If you found out you were near
      the end of your life,
      what unsaid words or unfinished
      deeds would you want to
      complete?

315. How many days in a year
      are extraordinarily good for you?

316. If you could leave one message
to the world on your tombstone,
what would it say?

(How about one message on your
spouse's tombstone?)

317. Finish this sentence:

Of the years I have lived,
this past one has been the most...

318. If you live to age seventy-five
you will have 657,000 hours in
your life.

Looking back over the past month,
which hour or two did you spend
most wisely?

319. What would it take to make you
      much happier than you are now?

320. How would you sum up your outlook
      on life in a one sentence motto?

321. If you met
      the wisest person in the world,
      what question would you ask?

322. Is the world around you any different
      because you have been here?

      How?

323. Rank the following in order
of importance to you,
highest to lowest:

Having all the money you desire.

A rewarding relationship
with your spouse and family.

Enjoyment and satisfaction at
work.

A good circle of personal friends.

324. What is your most inalienable right?

What freedom
do you value the most?

325. In your experience,
     which book have you enjoyed
     the most?

(No need to really answer this one!)

The strength of *What A Question!* lies in its diversity and breadth of subject matter. In the course of your conversations you've no doubt encountered many intriguing topics and questions. Would you like one of your questions to be included in a future New Voyage Books project? Write your question on the lines below and submit to: New Voyage Books, 415 Rt. 18, Suite 234, East Brunswick, NJ 08816

Please check if desired: [ ] If my question is accepted, please acknowledge my name as a contributor. Sorry, questions cannot be returned.

My question reads: _____

_____

_____

_____

_____

_____

_____

I understand that all copyright or other rights, if any, to this question or questions become the sole property of New Voyage Books upon receipt and that the question or questions may be used in future projects. I waive the right to any compensation in return for the use of my question or questions.

Signed _____ Date _____

DID YOU BORROW THIS BOOK?

WANT A COPY FOR A FRIEND OR LOVED ONE?

YES, I want ____ copies of *What a Question: Opening Doors To Conversation and Windows of Discovery.*

[ ] Check or money order enclosed

    Charge my [ ] Visa [ ] MasterCard

Account# _____ Exp. Date _____

Signature _____

Name _____ Phone _____

Address _____

City/State/Zip _____

    Enclose $7.95 plus $2.00 postage and handling per book. (New Jersey residents add $0.48 sales tax.) Canadian orders must be accompanied by a *postal money order in U.S. funds.* Allow 30 days for delivery. Make checks payable to: New Voyage Books, 415 Route 18, Suite 234, East Brunswick, NJ 08816

    Call (201)249-7569 for credit card orders

QUANTITY ORDERS INVITED

Call for quantity pricing or special UPS handling.